EXTRA ORDINARY

The distance between good and great

CORNELL THOMAS

outskirts
press

Extraordinary
The Distance Between Good and Great
All Rights Reserved.
Copyright © 2017 Cornell Thomas
v2.0

The opinions expressed in this manuscript are solely the opinions of the author and do not represent the opinions or thoughts of the publisher. The author has represented and warranted full ownership and/or legal right to publish all the materials in this book.

This book may not be reproduced, transmitted, or stored in whole or in part by any means, including graphic, electronic, or mechanical without the express written consent of the publisher except in the case of brief quotations embodied in critical articles and reviews.

Outskirts Press, Inc.
http://www.outskirtspress.com

ISBN: 978-1-4787-9078-5

Cover Photo © 2017 Kristen Rath Photography. All rights reserved - used with permission.

Outskirts Press and the "OP" logo are trademarks belonging to Outskirts Press, Inc.

PRINTED IN THE UNITED STATES OF AMERICA

Table of Contents

1. "C" 1
2. Seperation Anxiety 5
3. Try 9
4. Passion 13
5. Purpose 17
6. Ladders 20
7. One More Round 24
8. Cray-Cray 27
9. Hunger 30
10. Tina Thomas, The Great 33
11. I've Been There 36
12. Bryce 40
13. Niya 42
Original Quotes By Cornell Thomas 44
Acknowledgements 59

CHAPTER 1

"C"

I WILL NEVER forget the feeling of failure that spread throughout my body. As I slouched deep into my chair, I looked around to see if anyone else had caught site of the white piece of paper in front of me covered in red ink. This was not what I was expecting.

My mom thought I was a math genius. From first to sixth grade I could add, subtract, multiply, and divide, most times without the use of a calculator or my toes. I was fascinated with numbers, and Math was one of my favorite subjects, outside of lunch and gym. But there I sat, only a year removed from the sixth grade with a humongous "F" looking right back at me.

That year the numbers I loved so much were replaced with letters. 2 became X and 8 became Y. There was this weird new language called Algebra that I had to

EXTRAORDINARY

somehow learn to translate. That one failed test (in my mind) turned me from genius to gumshoe. I no longer had a passion for numbers. I decided that I would be retiring my calculator for good and from now on my only goal in Math was to reach the magical number of 70. Back then a score of 70 was a "C", and "C" was passing, so off I went on my journey to mediocrity.

My journey in Math isn't new or even unique. I'm sure there are millions of kids all over the world that feel like they just won the Super Bowl whenever they get a "C". It wasn't the grade that was so bad, it was the mindset I adopted because of it. Instead of gritting my teeth and giving everything I had to get better, I decided to quit before any actual work had to be done. I not only settled on being average, I accepted it. Words like *can't* and *try* became part of my everyday vocabulary when it came to my now least favorite subject.

There are billions of people on this planet that are happy with getting a "C" in life. They spend their days settling for ordinary when extraordinary is right around the corner.

As a speaker, I get the amazing opportunity to meet thousands of people from all over the world. My purpose is to help others, so I do a lot of listening and what I often hear takes me right back to my Math class. The same words I used in Math are echoed to me when these amazing people talk about their lives. "I can't possibly do that," "I guess I'll try it," or "what if I fail?" That mindset is why the Earth is filled with so many average people living average lives, until they hit the average age when people are supposed to cease existing.

Why did you pick up this book? Well, if you know me, and you did it because you love me, I appreciate it, but that isn't why I wrote it. I wrote this book to wake YOU the hell up. (Sorry for the cuss, Mom, but I'm fired up right now!) I have no regrets in life, not even my "failures" in Math, because I can look back at them now and promise myself I will never again have that mindset in anything else I do.

When you open my computer there's a picture of a lion looking right back at you. When you think like a lion you refuse to act like a sheep. You have to be stubborn enough to believe you can be great. You have to be stubborn enough to believe that with enough blood, sweat, and tears you can turn that "C" into an "A". And at the end of the day if all that work produced a "B", at least you can look at your life with no regrets. You put it all on the line and that's something most people don't have the courage to do.

On the cover of this book is my amazing son Bryce. When he was about a year old, whenever I opened

EXTRAORDINARY

my computer and he saw my screen saver he would roar, and every single time it made me proud. I never want him or my beautiful daughter, Niya, to accept defeat, especially the worst form of the word which is self-defeat.

If you're going to go out, my friends, make sure it's on your shield, not before the battle even starts.

CHAPTER 2

Seperation Anxiety

I DID A blog a while back called *Buddy Running*. It was a term I used coaching basketball when some of my players would pace each other while doing sprints. Now, if you're really observant and you noticed the words "pace" and "sprints" in the same sentence, congrats, you figured out what's wrong. You don't *pace* sprints; you run them as hard as you can. Since that is the case, I would always wonder why we would have a pack of players running at exactly the same speed. Shouldn't someone separate from the pack? Was it fear of leaving their buddy behind or was it fear of actually pushing themselves past their comfort zone?

Life tends to be the same way. The reason so many people are content with being average is because it's

EXTRAORDINARY

comfortable and easy. They don't want to make that extra push to be more. When you look to your left and right what do you see? Are you surrounded by people that make you better, or are you surrounded by people who are content staying the same? I don't look to my left and right because there's nobody there. I look forward because that's where my targets are. I have to give everything I have just to see them in the distance, but eventually I will catch up and replace them with new ones.

That's what the Great Ones do. Michael Jordan's goal growing up was to beat his brother, Larry, who used to absolutely punish him in basketball whenever they played 1 on 1. Once he started beating him convincingly, Jordan moved on to the next target, and the next one. I always say if there's no target in front of you, beware of the one on your back. When Jordan became the best player in the world, he found other ways to motivate himself. He wanted to put so much distance between himself and the next guy that there wouldn't be a discussion about who was the best player in the world. That's what separates the average from the good, and the good from the great.

So how do we separate ourselves from mediocre? How do you get out of the pack mentality? I will give you a trick I used to do with my buddy-runners. I would break up the pack using mental warfare. That sounds a little extreme as I'm re-reading this, but that's what needs to be done to change a mindset. I would say things like, "The first two players that win this next sprint are done running," then I would watch the whole pack miraculously dissipate. It was every man for himself. Out of nowhere, energy poured into their lifeless bodies and I suddenly had fifteen Usain Bolts in my gym.

Why is this trick so effective? Because that's exactly what it is: a trick. I'm tricking their minds by providing a finish line. After every sprint, another two guys would get a chance to rest. Nine times out of ten my players would find another gear somewhere inside them to get that break. We all have this reserve tank, it's just human nature, but there's something in us that waits for the finish line to unleash it.

So my question to you is, what's your finish line? Is it a big house? A fancy car? Your family living comfortably? What's going to make you separate yourself from the pack?

The fear of being average is enough to wake me up at 5am each morning. Now my newborn helps with that, as well, but knowing that I'm not where I want to be in life is what drives me to hunt for something more.

EXTRAORDINARY

Fear of what other people think can also be a factor in why you might be afraid to sprint ahead. Most of the Great Ones are considered outcasts or mavericks on the journey to becoming great. People will doubt your dreams, and that's okay as long as one of those people isn't you. My friends didn't understand how bad I wanted my dream of playing professional basketball because they are not me. If they knew what consumed my thoughts every day they would have probably staged an intervention.

It's ok to be the pariah, it's ok to chase what you want, and it's ok to let the flock fly past you as you go the other way. No snowflake was created the same, and the same holds true for us as human beings. We are all different. We're not meant to look the same, dress the same, talk the same, walk the same, have the same dreams, and run at the same speed. No one but you should ever determine the level on your life's treadmill. So get going in whatever direction you choose, the longer you wait, the farther the finish line becomes.

CHAPTER 3

Try

ONE OF MY least favorite words in the English Dictionary is the word *try*. *Try* to me is like getting an 8th place participation trophy when there were only 8 people competing. *Try* is a feeble way of putting a halfhearted effort into something. In this one word you can give yourself a million excuses. You hear the old saying, "Well, at least you tried," That is like nails on a blackboard for me. It's funny that people always "try" when it comes to doing something difficult. You never hear of people *trying* to eat a pizza, or *trying* to sleep in all day. Somehow they just do it. Average people *try* things, extraordinary people *do* them.

When you say try, you immediately give yourself an out. It's a way of only putting your toes in the swimming pool instead of actually jumping in. It's the fear of failure that usually makes most people try instead of do. What if I don't succeed? What if the girl/boy I ask out says no? What if? What if? What if? In every scenario failure is the expected outcome. You have to look at failure like great coaches look at losses. In every loss there's an opportunity for growth. I don't care how bad the loss (and I have been on the wrong side of some bad ones), once you get over your own pride there is always a take-away from each one.

This is how the truly great people on our planet view life. It's said that when Thomas Edison invented the light bulb he had over 10,000 failed experiments. When a reporter asked him how it felt to fail that many times (great question, jerk!) Edison replied, "I haven't failed, I just found 10,000 ways that won't work". It's hard for an average mind to understand that concept. That's why the distance between good and great seems light-years away for most people. I am here to tell you, developing that mindset is only as far away as you push it.

You might be thinking right now, "Why would I push that mindset away?" The answer is the same reason you *try* to do things, our old frienemie, Fear. Fear of what you might have to sacrifice to develop that kind of mindset. Fear that you might have to come out of that snug bubble you live in called your comfort zone. Fear has a funny way of talking us out of greatness, but you want to know the craziest thing about it? We control it. Fear is something we are conditioned with. It's a learned response. Which means we can unlearn it.

There's a huge difference between fear and danger. Danger is strapping steaks to your body and jumping into a lions' den yelling YOLO! That could also double as stupidity. Fear is not going to an audition because you heard that some really good actors are going out for the same part you want. This is the moment where the doers DO and the tryers move on to something else. I want you to do me a huge favor right now while you're reading this book. (Now if you're in the bathroom this might be a little difficult, but when you're done, wash your hands and answer this question. Seriously, please wash your hands. Okay, here we go.)

Answer the following question without hesitation, "What is scaring the absolute crap out of me (no pun intended) that could change my life for the better if I just did it?" Some of you will lie to me right now because it's hard to admit when something scares you. Self-assessment has to be honest. The only way you can change is by understanding that a change is needed. You're either all-in when it comes to chasing your dreams, or all-out, there is no in-between.

The next time you get to your swimming pool I want

EXTRAORDINARY

you to jump in. If you can't swim, by no means jump in, please put on the yellow ducky swimmies and start from the shallow end. I'm talking about anything you are attempting to try. No more *trying* my friends, just *do it!* And if, for whatever reason, you're not successful, learn the lesson and do it again!

CHAPTER 4

Passion

PASSIONATE PEOPLE STICK out in a crowd. They are usually the ones that wake up early and go to bed late. They have what seems to be an unlimited supply of energy. They aren't fueled by Dunkin Donuts, they are fueled by life. Passionate people have this contagious way of drawing others to them. After listening or talking to them for ten minutes you feel that you could tackle a bear, or maybe a small koala. (Don't try either one!)

I was never passionate about anything until I found basketball when I was 16 years old. I didn't know what love for anything outside of my family felt like. It's so hard to describe in words because it's an unexplainable feeling. My notebooks soon had scribbled drawings of basketballs all over them. I was like this obsessed stalker without the restraining order. I had access to my passion every day and I was the only thing that could limit that access. When I discovered what I thought I wanted to do for the rest of my life, it was hard to have a bad day because I knew my basketball would be waiting to cheer me up through the worst of times.

You can tell when you're passionate about something by the way you talk about it. When I discuss motivational speaking in front of people, my energy level naturally rises. It's like when two people argue about whose sports team is better, they are both passionate about their team and the next thing you know, the debate turns into an argument, or a silly bet that ends up with one of them streaking through the neighborhood. Life without passion isn't really much of a life at all.

The Great Ones are passionate. They have this zest for life that's contagious. Their passion triggers your emotions. I have watched inspirational speeches and have literally found myself laughing, crying, or looking for that small koala to tackle without even realizing it. Have you seen the last three minutes of "The Pursuit of Happiness"? Check out that clip on YouTube and tell me if it doesn't strike a chord. No, seriously, go do it now. I'm here for, like, another 9 chapters.

I'm always confused when people tell me they're not

PASSION

passionate about anything. They'll say things like, "There's really nothing that I want to do in life," or, "I just haven't found it yet." Now understand, the pursuit of finding your passion isn't always an easy journey. I didn't find mine until I was 16, and then I found a new one when I was 34. I wasn't born knowing what I wanted to do. The difference with me is, once I found it I didn't let it go.

Let's imagine a scenario right now. Close your eyes. Now ask yourself how the heck are you supposed to read the instructions with your eyes closed? Are you guys kidding me right now? Keep your eyes open and I will set the stage for you. We're going to start dreaming with our eyes open, ready? Okay, so imagine waking up every single day doing what you love more than anything else in this world. Some of you might be thinking of watching football, or being a desperate housewife. (Please, don't let the latter be it!) My point is, *that* is what living your passion feels like. Most people hate their alarm clock. I don't even own one. Every day I get up early because I'm excited to get up. I can't wait to start my day because I know it's going to be filled with things that I love. Would you dread getting out of bed if you knew whenever you woke up someone was going to give you a million dollars? Of course not!! There would be no wrong side of the bed; every side would feel amazing.

EXTRAORDINARY

I want to leave you with one simple equation:

Passion + Purpose = Power

When you have passion for life and know why you were created, nothing is impossible.

CHAPTER 5

Purpose

WHY ARE YOU here? Seriously, take a second and answer that question for me. If you think your life is just meant for you to exist and die, this book might not be for you. You have to believe that you have a purpose on this planet. Usually passion leads us directly to our purpose. Not convinced? Do you still think you're not here for any other reason?

Ok, tough guy, do this for me. Let's pretend you're going on a job interview for whatever profession you want. You get to the interview and you're informed that exactly 400 million other applicants have applied for the same position. Yeah that's right, *400 million* other people are going after the same job you want, and they want it just as much as you. You sit down and have a pretty good interview, but because you're human you start thinking there's no way you can beat out that many other people.

EXTRAORDINARY

As you back your Prius out of the parking lot to go home (You don't have a Prius?) your phone rings. The woman who just interviewed you informs you that, not only did you get the job, but you're starting next week. What would you be thinking? Probably that it's meant-to-be, right? It must be some type of divine intervention, correct? Well, that's exactly what happened for you to be born. You and about 450 million other swimmers competed to see who would be chosen to meet the lady that would uncomfortably hold you in her belly for the next 9 months, and guess what? You freaking won!! You beat all those other Michael Phelps wanna-bes and came into this world bright-eyed and bushy-tailed. If you came out with an actual tail that would be extremely awkward and your mom would have some explaining to do, but you know what I'm saying.

You have to first realize that you're here for a reason. Without grasping that simple concept you won't have any motivation to discover your purpose because why should you care? Second, you have to be able to see the signs the universe is sending your way. I saw the signs that basketball wasn't my true purpose before my injury; I just chose to ignore them. Your gut instincts have a funny way of usually being right; listen to them. If you wake up everyday feeling you're not doing what you were meant to do in this life, you're probably spot-on.

PURPOSE

The Great Ones know where they're going, even if they're not quite sure how they'll get there. I will give you a second to re-read that last sentence, seriously read it again. Knowing the WHY you're here doesn't immediately give you the HOW to make it happen. The blueprint is something you're going to have to work for and discover on your own. When I wanted to start spreading my message of positivity all over the world I didn't have a Sherpa helping me up the mountain. I researched, watched speakers that were already successful, and then carved out my own path to make it happen.

To be great, you have to DO. To be great, you have to BELIEVE that WHY you're here is so powerful, the HOW to make it happen will eventually lead you to formulate a plan. Do you remember the formula from last chapter? I'll wait while you check again. It's not like I gave you a Math equation, people. Yes, it's *Passion + Purpose = Power*. Without the second part of this equation the desired result will be a lot harder to achieve. Average folks just exist, you were meant for much, much more. You beat the odds just to get here, now continue to beat them and make the most of your life!

CHAPTER **6**

Ladders

I'VE NEVER BEEN a big fan of ladders. Before you start laughing, I want you to hear me out. First things first, my feet are huge and the little pieces of wood or metal I have to climb up were meant for people who get their sneakers at Baby Gap. Second, it usually requires someone else holding the ladder, which means my life is in someone else's hands and that thought never sits well with me. Lastly, it's hard to silence the *what if?* that is usually screaming inside my head. Like, *what if* I fall, *what if* this bee decides to sting me right now, or *what if* my size 15 sneakers get caught on the hobbit-sized rung and the old lady across the street decides to videotape it instead of calling 9-1-1, it goes viral, they call me "Ladder Daddy", and my fifteen minutes of fame eventually lands me on a D-list reality show with Screech and

LADDERS

Honey-Boo-Boo. Okay, I might have gone on a little bit of a tangent, but I'm back now.

My point is, the Great Ones look at ladders differently than normal folks. That's not saying the idea of falling isn't on their minds; I can assure you it is. The difference, my friends, is that their *what if* motivates, rather than debilitates them. They're able to use that fear of falling to help them climb. Fear is an amazing thing. I know you might be thinking I've officially lost my mind, but bear with me. Most people confuse fear with danger. Fear is saying to yourself that if you approach that lovely lady at the bar, she, her feminist friends, the bartender and everyone else, will point and laugh at your feeble pick up line. Danger is something completely different. It's usually when you're in a life threatening situation.and because we are human beings we often confuse the two.

Fear exists only in your mind. It is something that we have been conditioned with since we were born. Imagine attempting to break a thirty-year habit. It's not going to happen overnight for most people, but it's definitely doable. Fear can be your greatest weapon if you channel it properly. Instead of thinking about how far you'll drop off that ladder, imagine how high you can climb if you just go for it.

Average people, and even good ones, eventually

stop their ascent up the ladder for a number of reasons, if they even start the climb, at all. Some look down and are satisfied with how far they've already come. Others over-think the next step and get what's called paralysis by analysis. They end up frozen in place because they just don't believe in themselves enough to go any higher. Then you have the ones who could be great and have climbed pretty high only to become comfortable with where they are, allowing self-satisfaction to make them forget there are always more stairs to climb. In sports we call this "getting fat" off your wins. Once you feel you've arrived, your work ethic starts to suffer. Do you fall into any of these categories?

Did you not see your option on that list? That's a good thing because it means you're always climbing. It's okay to take a short break and admire how far you've come, but if you want to truly be great, that break will only be a pit stop. The Great Ones are life-long learners. They know there is always another level up ahead. I make it a point to learn something new every day, from all different kinds of people.

You could be asking yourself, "What if I climb all the way up the ladder only to discover it's not the one I should be on?" My answer to that is very simple: Climb down and find the right one for you. Personally, I have been on three different ladders in my lifetime.

LADDERS

One as a basketball player, one as a coach, and now the one I'm climbing as a speaker, author, and world-changer. I know my current ladder has no ceiling, but I'm more than willing to see how far it goes.

CHAPTER 7

One More Round

OUR SOCIETY HAS a fascination with the underdog. We seek out stories of people that have overcome insurmountable odds to win in the end. Why is that? I believe it's because the underdog gives us hope. It makes us look at our own lives and think, "If they can do it, why can't I?"

One of the biggest cinematic underdog stories of all time was the "Rocky" series. It had all the elements of a prototypical comeback story. Down on his luck hero that doesn't know his potential, wise old trainer that believes in him (although not initially), superior adversary that he must defeat to win. Does that formula sound familiar? Of course it does, insert any underdog movie you want and you will see the same story line.

What I love about underdog movies is a trait most

of the main characters possess. They REFUSE to quit and that's what eventually makes them great. Quitting is not in their D.N.A. You can knock Rocky down a million times, but you know he's getting back up on wobbly legs to keep fighting. Now let's make something clear here, I'm not saying there aren't moments when they quit temporarily. I'm also not saying there aren't moments of doubt. That, my friends, is called human nature. But these heroes never succumb to the disease called quitting, and that's exactly what it is, a disease.

Quitting starts in the mind and spreads throughout the whole body. Once you think you can't run anymore, do another squat, write another report, etc., your mind becomes engaged in this mini boxing match. It becomes you versus this humungous adversary, also called you. Your mind starts this internal battle for your body. On one side there is a voice telling you to push through, saying that you can do this; and on the other side, your mind is saying you can't take anymore, or your hear, "Forget this, lets go get a pizza."

The Great Ones have a no-quit mentality. It's not typically something that's inherited; it's earned through getting up off the canvas over and over again. The more you get knocked down, the more you work on getting back off your arse (I was in England once). There's a vast difference between getting knocked

EXTRAORDINARY

down and staying down. Make sure you can distinguish between the two.

I've said in previous books that your mind is your strongest muscle. You build it through your experiences, both good and bad. When we fall as kids, what do our parents say? Do they let us stay down on the floor crying? No! The first thing they say is, "Get up and wipe yourself off." So why do we tend to forget that important life lesson as we get older?

When you get older, Mommy and Daddy aren't there to dust off your corduroys and pat you on the head; you have to do it yourself. The ability to get up after being knocked down is a trait that all the Great Ones possess. It would be tough to find a successful person that hasn't been knocked down their fair share of times. The difference, my friends, is they refuse to stay down.

CHAPTER 8

Cray-Cray

I'M CRAZY ENOUGH to think that everything I want to accomplish will eventually happen. I'm crazy enough to believe that I will change the world for the better. I'm crazy enough to go to bed late and wake up early in the constant pursuit of my dreams. I'm crazy enough to bet on me, no matter what the odds. I'm crazy enough to be so passionate about my mission that I will jump before the net appears. Yes, I'm crazy. As a matter-of-fact, I'm cray-cray, and I believe that's even crazier than crazy.

You see, the Great Ones have to be crazy. Normal people have normal ambitions because their minds are confined to their comfort zones. Being crazy isn't "normal" so why would they want to be that? Why would they want to take chances? Why would they strive to be more? No one else is doing it, so why should they break the mold?

EXTRAORDINARY

If you look at the people on our planet that are truly great, you will notice that almost every single one of them has the crazy gene ingrained in their DNA. This past year I went to a Tony Robbins seminar to see one of the best in my profession. I wanted to soak in all the knowledge I possibly could. Although Tony dropped a knowledge bomb on me the size of Texas that week, one of my biggest take-aways from the event was that this man is absolutely out of his mind, in the best possible way.

For six nights in a row, I watched this human being speak from 12pm to 1:30am with essentially no breaks. After the first day, I assumed something would eventually have to give, be it his bladder or his energy, but I was wrong on both counts. This dude brings it every second he is on that stage. At some point I had to ask myself a very important question, "Cornell, are you crazy enough?"

When I decided to play basketball instead of going to both my junior and senior proms, people probably thought I was crazy, but it was normal to me. That's what's so difficult for most people to comprehend. People like Tony Robbins and Michael Jordan are just being who they are. Their *crazy* is completely normal to them.

Being extraordinary isn't determined by financial

success alone. It's about not accepting average. It's about fighting through the storm even when there aren't any immediate signs of it passing. Who you are during times of turmoil determines who you end up eventually becoming. Life isn't easy. Things happen that take an extraordinary amount of grit and mental toughness to get through.

To me, crazy is not believing that you have a purpose; it's not realizing that whatever you really want, you can have if you're willing to work for it. You see, I could stop chasing my dreams. I could go work a "normal" 9 to 5 job and not follow my passion or accomplish my life's mission, but for me, my friends, that is just crazy.

CHAPTER 9

Hunger

IN MY LIFETIME, to-date, I can honestly say I have never met anyone that uses as many analogies for life as my mother. Some are hilarious, but always insightful; my mom always had a way of spinning her message. Sometimes she would use popular ones like, "Birds of a feather flock together," but mostly she would create her own on the fly.

One day early in my basketball career my mom told me to treat the basketball like a biscuit. I started smiling immediately before trying to figure out what she was actually saying. I was so busy imagining myself slam dunking a biscuit that I didn't catch the other part of the sentence, until I stopped laughing (in my mind, of course.) What my mom was saying was that I needed to treat the game of basketball like it was not just food, but the last piece of food on this earth.

She wanted me to understand that if I wanted to be successful at basketball, I had to be hungry. I had to act like that darn basketball was the only thing keeping me alive, and I had to do whatever I had to do to make sure nothing took it away from me.

Think about that. Imagine if you treated your dreams and goals like it was your only food source. Imagine how hungry you would be to protect those dreams and how hard you would go after them.

One of my favorite speakers is Les Brown, and one of his famous phrases is, "You got to be Hungry." Hunger is such a great description for chasing your dreams because when you're hungry, you're willing to do whatever it takes to eat. You see thousands of homeless people all over the world in the middle of busy streets, carting their lives around in the dead of winter to find a good location to ask for help, just so they can eat.

When you're hungry there is no *I'll do it tomorrow*, because there might not be a tomorrow. When I started to look at the game of basketball like that, I never took it for granted again because I knew it was the only thing (at that time) that I had. It was my way to college; it was my way to help change our financial situation at home; it was everything.

EXTRAORDINARY

The same mentality I had back then is the same one I have now, but my biscuit is no longer basketball, it's serving others and spreading my message of positivity to help make the world a better place.

The reverse of being hungry is being full. How different are those two sensations? When you're full, all you want to do is sit and sleep. Being full is when people feel they have "arrived" and there's no more work to be done.

The Great Ones know they never actually arrive, they always stay hungry. If you played Michael Jordan in a game of Uno right now, you would assume he was going to rip your heart out because he would play with the same ferocity and hunger as he did when he was playing basketball.

Never lose your hunger for greatness; the moment you feel you have arrived is the moment your hunger departs. Stay hungry!!

CHAPTER **10**

Tina Thomas, The Great

MOM, I'M NOT quite sure how to start this chapter. It's not that I have writer's block or there isn't enough material about you in my heart to fill these pages. The problem is that I want to make sure these words don't do you a disservice. My skills as a writer pale in comparison to your ability as a mother. This book is about being extraordinary, and there is no better example of that word than you, Mom.

You raised a dreamer. I think you knew this even when I was a little boy, but even I struggle with understanding how you did it. How did you raise 5 kids by yourself? How did you make us feel that we had everything, even on the days when we had nothing? How did you show us your beautiful smile on the outside when inside there must have been days that you felt like crying? How did you do it, Mom?

EXTRAORDINARY

That question sometimes comes into my mind when I watch you play with Bryce and Niya. I watch how you navigate the rough waters of diapers and tantrums with a smile on your face. I watch how Bryce and Niya look at their Nana with such love in their eyes, and then it finally hits me. My mom is a superhero! Not the ones that fight crime in tights and a cape, but the ones that accomplish the extraordinary on a daily basis without even thinking about it.

These are the people that run into burning buildings to save a stranger they have never met. These are the people that teach kids solely because of the love they have for their students. These are the people that volunteer their time to serve others in need because their hearts compel them to. These people are you, Mom. You are my superhero.

The reason I can't figure out how you did it, is the same reason no one can quite figure out that the only difference between Clark Kent and Superman is a cheap pair of bifocals. You are on a different level, Mom. You are truly extraordinary.

Every day I thank God for giving me you. Right now I'm in a public place typing this chapter while trying to hold back the tears that want to run down my face. They're not tears of sadness, they are tears of gratitude. Despite not having all the materialistic things that other kids had growing up, my siblings and I were the lucky ones. We got a gift that no money could ever buy. We got you.

You taught me to never idolize another human being, and you will be proud to know that I never have, with one exception. I am who I am because you are who you are, and I just want to thank you for being extraordinary.

I Love You,

Your Babyboy

CHAPTER **11**

I've Been There

I KNOW DESPITE all the information you've received in this book you're still hesitant. You're hesitant to adopt this mindset into your everyday life. You're afraid to sacrifice your comfort zone to chase the unknown. You don't want to veer off that broad highway of normalcy that leads to nowhere, for fear that you might never find it again in case you fail. I just want to tell you one thing. I've been there.

Right now I'm using the Wi-Fi from a local Starbuck's because I haven't been able to afford the Internet in our house for the last month. In my car I have a bag full of change to bring to the bank for gas money for the week. I have checked and refreshed my online bank account praying that money comes in to clear checks that I've written to pay bills. I've been there.

I'VE BEEN THERE

I went to the Tony Robbins event (in Boca Raton, Florida) with $100 dollars to my name and prayed that I would have enough money to get through the week. I've looked at a negative bank account and wondered what I need to do just to get it up to zero. I've been there. I know what you're going through, but there's a difference.

I'm not planning on staying here. I'm not going to live in a negative mindset. If you have this book in your hands and it's past March 11, 2017 it means we have already had our very first Positivity Summit. It was a movement I started because I was just crazy enough to believe I could make a difference. You're looking at a man that has gone through the storm, and here he stands right in front of you, bruised but not broken, to tell his story. You're looking at a man that never quit no matter how bad the cards were stacked against him. You're looking at a man that was raised to fight through adversity, not collapse because of it. But when it's all said and done, you're just looking at a man. A man with the same physical limitations as you. A man who is human, just like you. A man who needed to convince himself, just like you, that he could be great. A man who has seen what the bottom floor looks like and decided to find the elevator.

What I want you to know is that anything is possible.

EXTRAORDINARY

It's going to take some pain to get to your purpose; it's going to take some grit to weather some of the storms coming your way; but from that struggle, my friends, comes your greatness.

BONUS CHAPTERS

CHAPTER **12**

Bryce

TO MY FIRST born. Bryce, I will never forget holding you in my arms as the nurse told me your measurements. Mom was still in surgery and it was just us boys at 4:28am, meeting for the first time. I knew you were a boy before your mom was even showing. I know that's going to sound a little weird so I'll explain it further. One of your grandfathers was a man by the name of Bobby Thomas. He was my father, and your initials are the same as his for a reason. Your grandfather passed away when I was only four years old but he left footprints on this earth that can still be seen today.

Bobby Thomas helped countless numbers of people in the city of Passaic where your dad was first raised. His mission in life was to give back and serve others. He was faithful to that mission until his very last day on earth. The reason I'm telling you this, Son, is because your dad is the same way. You'll see it as you get older, but your father loves helping people and has chosen the same mission as his father before him.

I don't know what you'll want to be in life when you get older, but giving back is in your DNA. Whatever you choose to do, Son, do it with passion. Never forget to help others (especially your little sister and your amazing mom) and always remember to treat others as you would want to be treated.

Not everyone will appreciate you, not everyone will embrace you, and not everyone will understand you, and that's fine. Just never, ever stop believing in yourself. When you have a dream (regardless of the odds) put everything into it and make it happen. Your father's dream is to change the world for the better. I did that when you and your sister were born. I love you, Bubba. Thank you for making my dreams come true.

CHAPTER 13

Niya

TO MY LITTLE princess: One thing you probably will learn about your daddy is he'll never lie to you. So it would be wrong to say that I wasn't wrapped around your finger as soon as I laid eyes on you. Niya, much like your amazing mother, there's a light inside you that people will gravitate toward immediately. Your smile stops me in my tracks. In the ten months you've been on this earth, I've must have kissed you ten million times (possibly more.) Niya, the world will try and convince you not to be strong. It will tell you that women are supposed to look and act a certain way. I want you to know that you were not created to be like everyone else.

You were not designed to be average, Baby. Like your big brother, you were designed for greatness. Never

NIYA

think you have to dim your light because others can't handle your shine. You are not going to nicely conform to the cookie-cutter image that most people think women should fit into. If Bryce and I ever allow you to date (maybe at 40?), your husband will know that he married a lioness. A strong, beautiful, independent, intelligent, and proud woman that will not stand behind him, but will be proud to walk by his side. Niya, you are the most beautiful thing I've ever seen, inside and out. Never, ever forget that. I love you, Baby. Oh, and listen to your older brother, he's protective because he loves you!!

Original Quotes By Cornell Thomas

Fall in love with the process and you'll never regret the product.

You can't swim towards your dreams if you're drowning in doubt.

Your talk should always match your walk.

At the end of the day it's how you see yourself that determines your success or failure.

Legacy is often forgotten by those who don't remember that what you give will always be more important than what you have.

With ignorance comes division with education comes harmony.

ORIGINAL QUOTES BY CORNELL THOMAS

Don't expect more unless you're willing to do more.

You're not the only one after your dream; do you really want to wait to go for it?

Forgetting the past is almost as bad as living in it.

It's hard to design your present life without your past blueprint, learn and move on.

Giving a dollar pales in comparison to giving your time, choose wisely.

You can wait on opportunity or go out and make it.

Those who can't see your path should never choose your direction.

You can't change the game without playing it.

Life is a gift don't waste it by not living the one you want.

Negative words should be a speed bump not a roadblock against your positive actions.

Your problem isn't the problem how you address it is.

Opportunity won't matter for the unprepared.

EXTRAORDINARY

The more you practice quitting the easier it becomes.

The bigger the dream the bigger the action that needs to be done to make it happen.

Being present is the greatest present you could ever give.

No one has ever been enamored by the beauty of a skeleton, looks have an expiration date kindness does not.

Who you were is the only thing that stays behind when we pass away.

Opportunity is created not given.

Every today we have the opportunity to fight for a better tomorrow, never give up.

Never base the merits of a lion on the opinions of a sheep.

The open mind is an opportunity waiting to happen.

Don't get lost in a loss, learn the lesson and be grateful for the blessing.

Our connection is imperfection.

ORIGINAL QUOTES BY CORNELL THOMAS

Don't manifest mediocrity; see the greatness to be the greatness.

Your mission is greater than the opposition.

Adversity is a chapter in the story not the whole book, turn the page.

There will never be a way if you stop looking today.

The road you're going is a reflection of the seeds you're sowing.

Imagine what would be possible if you never heard of the word impossible.

You can either drown in the process or swim to victory.

Those that constantly complain are bound to stay the same.

Show your gratitude with your attitude, appreciate each moment.

Nothing changes without action.

Never judge the book by the color of the cover.

Fear will stop as many dreams as you allow.

EXTRAORDINARY

It's easy to find light in the sun, the clouds may hide but only you can make it disappear.

You're the engine fear can be your fuel or your failure.

Life is a bunch of moments make sure you take advantage of each one.

Success isn't the absence of struggle it's moving forward despite it.

You were meant to be great you just don't know it yet.

Opportunity often comes with sacrifice you have to give in order to get.

Allow yourself to be yourself.

If you want to see which friends are true have a different point of view.

It's hard to be loved if you're unwilling to give it.

You are a testament of your tribulations scars don't break you they make you.

The stress is only a test no good story has a smooth road.

ORIGINAL QUOTES BY CORNELL THOMAS

You can run from the challenge or run through it.

So many make the decision to never discover their mission, find your purpose.

Your support system can't have you missing, have faith in you and others will too.

Without passion your product will never prosper love what you do and others will too.

If you let others speak for you you'll never find your voice.

Time is currency make sure you're spending it on what's valuable to you.

Never let the opposition deter you from the opportunity.

The dream is irrelevant without the belief and action to achieve it.

Nothing will stop you faster than you, there will always be fear when the dream is near.

Looking past the past only helps you repeat it, take notes before you move on.

Your struggle is only a chapter not the whole story, eventually the page will turn.

EXTRAORDINARY

Even the worst card in the deck can still be played, don't quit the game because of what you're dealt.

If you're not where you want to be work for the life you want to see.

The anticipation of the destination should fuel the journey.

Every storm has an expiration date make sure your will does not.

Never conform because it's the norm, we weren't meant to be the same.

Worrying about what others say is an effective way to waste the day.

As long as you have your fight there's light, quitting is when the darkness comes.

Don't chase the ones into your life that are trying to run out of it.

It's shocking how many closed minds have such open mouths.

When your doubt exceeds your do start believing in something greater than you.

ORIGINAL QUOTES BY CORNELL THOMAS

Opportunity doesn't know when you're ready so always be prepared for it.

You're only as tough as your next challenge.

The biggest loss in the game of life is the one you refused to learn from.

You can look back without living back; the future is in front of you not behind you.

There will never be an end to the journey each step unlocks a new beginning.

Not everyone will match motivation with movement just make sure you do.

Doubt is contagious don't let others infect you with it.

Ignoring the problem only allows it time to grow.

Even an open book has hidden chapters, do your research.

With success comes risk you're going to have to pay to play.

A path without obstacles will surely lead you to a goal without merit.

EXTRAORDINARY

Quitting is a habit that gets easier with practice change your routine.

Change cannot happen through complacency, action is required.

Faith has a funny way of not forgetting those that have not forgotten it.

Trust life's timing it will happen if you will it to.

Feeding yourself lies will always keep you empty.

Your power has yet to be discovered, you have more in the tank then you think.

Veto your ego the man who knows it all knows nothing.

Danger and fear do a great job at having people mistake one for the other.

The most positive voice in your life should be your own.

Every miss is an opportunity to learn for your next make.

To catch a dream you have to decide between being comfortable or courageous.

ORIGINAL QUOTES BY CORNELL THOMAS

Nothing can stop an unstoppable mind.

If you can't find your passion start looking for your purpose.

Preparation is fears worst enemy, prepare for the moment and you won't shrink in it.

Trust in the process is crucial for the product.

The magic of the dream is the work put into accomplishing it.

Never misdiagnose me with the disease of conformity.

Keep a healthy distance between your dreams and those that doubt them.

Change is a product of vision and action you must see what needs to be done and then do it.

There will always be a disgrace in every race don't be fooled by fools.

A closed mind rarely opens long enough to learn the truth.

Life will always be what you believe it to be.

EXTRAORDINARY

Not all obstacles are meant to break you, thank the struggle for the strength.

Positivity and Negativity are always fighting for your attention choose wisely.

Whoever you pretend to be you'll never be, stay true to you.

It's hard to appreciate a new day while dwelling on old problems.

Never let anyone's negative words stop your positive actions, there will always be one.

Adversity has an amazing way of introducing us to who we truly are.

Never defend your character to characters.

You would be amazed how many choose to live in life's maze, find your own direction.

Sometimes you have to find comfort in the chaos before you can overcome it.

Your potential will rest on your passion, your purpose, and your persistence.

ORIGINAL QUOTES BY CORNELL THOMAS

There's magic in the moment be still and embrace it.

Be thankful for all no matter how big or small gratitude depends on attitude.

A kind word can change a life make sure to share them abundantly.

Listening to the negative voice is completely your choice.

It's your time when you decide to stop convincing yourself it isn't.

Life is the art of bending with the bad times without breaking despite them.

A better version of you should begin with each day that is new.

Step away from the problem to find the solution, if you can't the problem might be you.

In times of triumph never forget the trials of adversity that led you there.

Faith is knowing that your next win is hidden in your current loss, believe my friends.

EXTRAORDINARY

The only guarantee in life is how you choose to live it.

Love will take you as far as you allow it to.

No matter how hard the battle you still have more fight left inside you, get up.

Faith has a funny way of turning the impossible into possible.

Never believe in a statistic more than you believe in yourself.

Words can change thoughts but action can change lives, give without wanting to get.

Your life is a gift never return it by not living it to the fullest.

The fight isn't over until you submit to it!

Remember that taking a stand often requires getting up after being knocked down.

Knowing thyself is your greatest wealth.

Division is the subtraction of empathy and understanding and the addition of hate and ignorance.

ORIGINAL QUOTES BY CORNELL THOMAS

Picking up the pieces is required to solve any puzzle especially the one called life.

Everyone has a fight worth fighting for.

Gratitude is the repetition of recalling all you have when all seems lost.

Solitude is a component of success.

Things will always stay the same if you do, change takes action.

Your happiness will always be your responsibility.

All the support you need is sometimes just waiting in the mirror.

Fear will always supply the excuse you're looking for.

Your time is the exact moment you realize it has always been.

You need to disconnect in order to reconnect, be human.

Your negative emotion makes you human living in it makes you insane.

EXTRAORDINARY

Be stubborn enough to not allow yourself to quit.

We are all under construction don't give up on the blueprint before you break ground.

Positivity and negativity need momentum to grow make sure you're feeding the right one.

Defeat is part of the journey to victory, learn from it.

Love is the bridge between hate an understanding.

You can pity your past or prosper despite it, the choice is yours.

Don't waste days waiting for a new year to get better, save time do it now.

Being kind is free take advantage of it.

The pursuit of your purpose will take patience embrace the journey.

Acknowledgements

I would like to first thank my mother Tina Thomas for making her only dream in life to be raising her kids the right way. Thanks mom for all your sacrifice we love you more than words can express. I would like to thank my amazing wife Melissa for supporting a dream chaser no matter how outrageous the dream, and for being the best mom in the world hands down. (I'm biased) I want to thank my son Bryce who not only graced this cover, but for being daddy's best friend and adventure partner. I would also like to thank my beautiful daughter Niya (your cover is coming soon baby) for making me smile everyday, and melting me with a look. I want to thank my west coast mom and mother in law Janice Mitchell for your love. I would like to thank my brothers who have influenced me each in their own way. Ron for being the father figure in our lives. Robert for coming into our lives and becoming such a great mentor to me. Craig for helping me understand that being different is a good thing and should be celebrated. Romont for making me tougher through our secret battles that mom couldn't know about. Tony for being a fellow dreamer. My little sister Alicia the world traveler/princess and my older sister Jackie. I would like to also thank my brother in law Andy, and super talented sister in law Jamilia, welcome to our crazy (in a great way) family. I would also like to thank my beautiful niece Tiana, my amazing nephew Nasir and mi bella niece Leila.

I want to thank all my aunts, uncles and family that have shown me love throughout my life, and my big cousin Carlos for inspiring me to pick up a basketball. My Crossroads Basketball family thank you for helping me find my purpose I love you all for not only believing in what we do but how we do it. Cant forget my two generals at Crossroads Basketball Vinny Synol and Randy Jackson you guys are the epitome of what we're about thank you for all that you do. Thanks to the wonderful Vicki White for editing my masterpiece I love you mom. Thanks to Mr. Enthusiasm Robert E Criner for the wonderful forward and being a great mentor. Thanks to Renzo Gracie for being an amazing and inspiring person on and off mats. Thanks to George Sernack for bringing jiujitsu into my life. Thanks to all my brothers and sisters from RWMMA and NJMMA. A big thanks to my extended family Renzo Gracie NYC. Shout out to all the dancing bears especially my brothers Ryan and Marlon, to my little

ACKNOWLEDGEMENTS

sister Day Day, professor Ze, and far to many people to name, love you guys.

To the Mantegna family and my Blair Academy family. The Stafford family, Hayes family, Kniffin family, Cavanaugh Family, Feltus Family, Korn Family, Lord Family, Ledesma Family, Faubert Family, Muller Family, Goldsberry Family, Baranowski Family, Abrahamsen Family, DeMasi Family, Breheny Family, Colston Family, Garay Family, Smith Family, Livingston Family, Pinsonault Family, D'Alessio family, Synol Family, Jackson Family, Endicott family, Hart Family from UK, Walters Family, Kennedy Family, Civello Family, My Q Kettlebell Family, Padden family and my publicist/sis Ally Padden. Skip, Leah, Cam, and T from the UK, Spillane Family, Denville Pharmacy Crew, Heather Gogo and her party of 6, Dara my starbucks buddy, Rachel Weinrich, Rebecca Kay, Population Unplugged, Givnin family, Bertram Family, Quimby Family, BIG Womens Group, Staci and Danny V, The Laguardias and the Stuckey Chiropractic Crew. All my network marketers worldwide. The good people at Urwa,, and countless others that have helped me throughout this process. My Oola family for inspiring me daily. Rich M King, Elizabeth, and my Sherman Oakes crew (Chip,LA and any barrister from starbucks) And a big shoutout to my sis Tracey Edmonds from Alright TV.

EXTRAORDINARY

To my social media crew Maria Giacalone Sinclair, Ntellekt, Impowerr, Alex and Ani, Mia Praught, Tony Robbins, Annie Hawkins. KK from Uk, Aussie Jocelyn, Danielle Martin, Shelly, Robyn, Barry, Ike, Missy and my LA crew. Beebe Family, Di Di from LA, Lemasters from Ark, Katrina, Juanita, June Archer, Tim Forty, Deidre Breakenridge, Jillian Lyoden, Elaine Williams, Cornel West, and my Positivity Summit Crew!!!

A special thanks to Kristen Rath Photography for their unbelievable work and patience on the cover, and author photo. And also the amazing Alicia for her touch up work on the cover thanks my friend!!

This page wouldn't be complete if I didn't save the last spot for my two fathers. Bobby Thomas despite only being alive for my first four years on earth, you have inspired me throughout my life with the countless stories of how much you gave back to the community of Passaic, and to those less fortunate. Your footprints are too big to follow so I will do my best to walk right beside them. My second dad Steve Mitchell, a real life cowboy in every since of the word. You accepted me with open arms and gave me your blessing to marry your daughter. I know the two of you are smiling down at your grandson Bryce, I love you with all my heart.

ACKNOWLEDGEMENTS

There are a million other people that I want to individually thank but I can't let the acknowledgement page be longer than the book, I love you all thank you!!

CPSIA information can be obtained
at www.ICGtesting.com
Printed in the USA
FFOW05n0112090817